GW00673467

WOKING TO PORTSMOUTH

Vic Mitchell and Keith Smith

MP Middleton Press

Cover picture: By October 1968, steam had ceased at Guildford but the water column remained. The first generation of electric trains were at retirement age and the declining freight traffic was diesel-hauled, but the station was still intact. (J. Scrace)

Published 1985
First reprint June 1996
First reprint August 2003

ISBN 0 906520 25 8

Design   Deborah Esher
Typesetting   Barbara Mitchell

Published by
   Middleton Press
   Easebourne Lane
   Midhurst, West Sussex
   GU29 9AZ
Tel: 01730 813169
Fax: 01730 812601
Email: enquiries@middletonpress.fsnet.co.uk

Printed & bound by Biddles Ltd, Kings Lynn

CONTENTS

Bedhampton	109
Buriton Siding	92
Farncombe	35
Fratton	112
Godalming New	42
Godalming Old	38
Guildford	14
Haslemere	57
Havant	103
Hilsea	110
Liphook	64
Liss	71
Milford	46
Peasmarsh Junction	33
Petersfield	83
Portsmouth Harbour	117
Portsmouth & Southsea	114
Rowlands Castle	97
Witley	51
Woking	1
Woodcroft Halt	96
Worplesdon	11

ACKNOWLEDGEMENTS

We would like to thank all those mentioned in the photograph credits for the assistance we have received and our gratitude also goes to I. Baker, J. Barrett, Mrs. E. Fisk, J.B. Horne, S. Grout, N. Langridge, R. Randell, N. Stanyon, R.C. Riley, R. Stevenson, R.D. Smith and our ever helpful wives.

GEOGRAPHICAL SETTING

Like other lines from the Thames Valley to the South Coast, the route crosses both the North Downs and the South Downs. The former is almost at its narrowest where the line pierces it, by means of two short tunnels, close to the Wey Gap and just south of Guildford. Thereafter the railway begins a climb onto the high ground of the Lower Greensand of the Western Weald for over 20 miles, apart from one brief dip onto Weald clay south of Witley. Near Petersfield, the line begins a steep climb onto the South Downs, passing through a tunnel at the top of the scarp slope. Thereafter there is a lengthy and beautiful descent, along one of the many chalkland dry valleys, before reaching the coastal plain.

HISTORICAL BACKGROUND

Portsmouth's first service was a branch from the London - Southampton railway to Gosport, opened in 1841 by the London & South Western Railway. Portsmouth passengers had to suffer the double inconvenience of crossing the harbour entrance on the chain ferry and travelling through the town of Gosport, the terminal station being over 1/2 mile from the ferry. The lack of direct rail access put Portsmouth at a disadvantage with Southampton, particularly hampering its development as a port. The situation improved with the westward extension of the London, Brighton & South Coast Railway from Brighton to Portsmouth in 1847. The precise dates are shown on the map. It involved the penetration of the substantial military defences on the northern shore of Portsea Island and the provision of drawbridges. The LSWR had been planning its own direct line to Portsmouth from Fareham, but owing to financial difficulties and the £12,000 demanded by the Board of Ordnance for a further penetration of the defences, arrangements were made with the LBSCR for the line between Cosham and Portsmouth to be jointly owned. Thus from the Autumn of 1848, passengers from Portsmouth to London had the choice of two equally circuitous routes – via Brighton or via Eastleigh. Whilst this equitable arrangement suited the railway companies, it was not popular with the travelling public.

Another early branch from the London - Southampton railway was that from Woking to Guildford, which opened in 1845. It was extended to Godalming in 1849, the year in which the South Eastern Railway reached Guildford from Redhill.

As the LSWR and LBSCR were content to leave the situation as it was, it was left to an independent group, led by the well known railway contractor, Thomas Brassey, to obtain an Act of Parliament in 1853 to construct a direct line. The 32¾ mile single line from Godalming to Havant was constructed speculatively. (The original terminus at Godalming remained in use until 1897). The LSWR was the obvious customer but they were reluctant to use it for fear of antagonising the LBSCR. However, they were forced to lease it to prevent the SER from gaining control.

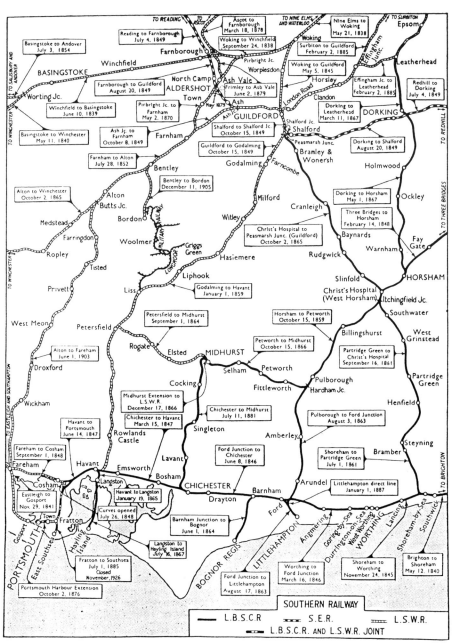

(Railway Magazine)

The inevitable confrontation occurred, first in Court and then at Havant on 28th December 1858, when the LBSCR physically prevented a LSWR train proceeding by the removal of rails and the blocking of the line with an engine. This event has been over-dramatically described as the Battle of Havant (although one driver was forcibly ejected from his engine). Temporary bus services and further court actions were necessary before regular services commenced on 8th August 1859.

In the 1860s, extensions were laid to Portsmouth dockyard and to Southsea Pier, although the latter was a horse-worked street tramway. It later became the nucleus of the Corporation Tramways network.

In the mid 1860s, a railway was built southwards from Havant to Hayling Island. It is fully described and illustrated in our *Branch Line to Hayling.*.

The Portsmouth terminus had been built on the outside of the Inner Defences and it was to be nearly 30 years before those responsible for national security would accept that they were obsolete. Thus it was not until 2nd October 1876 that the one-mile extension to the Harbour station was opened by the joint Committee, bringing passenger trains, at last, to the berths of the Isle of Wight and Gosport ferries. To the south of the new terminus a branch was provided to the Gun Wharf and, to the north, a second line to the Dockyard was constructed.

The doubling of the "contractor's line" was completed on 1st March 1878. The other landmark in the line's history was 4th July 1937 when electric services were introduced.

London and South Western Ry.
———
787
TO
GUILDFORD

1″ scale map of 1885.

PASSENGER SERVICES

The following notes relate to services between Guildford and Havant.

Initially, four trains were provided each way, only one of which carried third class passengers. By 1869, the frequency had increased to five (but only three on Sundays) with an additional eight trains running to Godalming Old station. In 1890, the basic weekday through service was seven journeys, with an extra trip between Waterloo and Petersfield. Godalming Old, by then, had 10 weekday and 6 Sunday departures and arrivals.

A slow but steady increase in traffic resulted in 17 through trains operating on weekdays in 1924 (11 on Sundays) with 5 journeys south to Petersfield. By this time there were two through trains on Sundays between Midhurst and Portsmouth.

Electrification brought a dramatic improvement in frequency, with two slow and one fast trains per hour. On summer Saturdays and Sundays this was increased up to six trains per hour each way. During WWII, the basic service was largely maintained, although devoid of restaurant cars in the latter years.

In 1970, the basic service was amended to give one fast, one semi-fast and one slow each hour. The 1977 timetable showed only two trains per hour but owing to strong protestations from railwayman and travellers alike, the cuts were never implemented.

Cross country tains were introduced by the Southern Railway – for example Deal to Bournemouth via Guildford. BR enterprisingly commenced a service between Manchester and Portsmouth in 1982 and also one between Leeds and Portsmouth (north on Friday afternoons and south on Sunday evenings). Although the latter service survives in 1985, the former inexplicably and uselessly operates between Portsmouth and Poole via Reading.

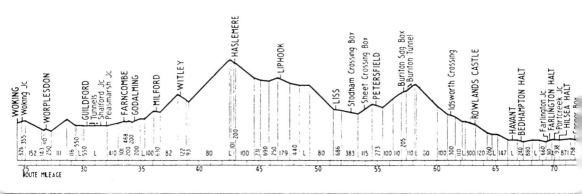

THROUGH EXPRESS SERVICE

BETWEEN

DEAL, FOLKESTONE, DOVER, MARGATE, etc.,

AND

SOUTHAMPTON, BOURNEMOUTH, etc.,

Via GUILDFORD.

CORRIDOR CARRIAGES.

Week Days only.			Week Days only.		
		a.m.			a.m.
Deal.. .. ..dep.		9 10	Bournemouth { West ..dep.		10 36
Walmer .. .. ,,		9 15	{ Central .. ,,		10 48
Dover Priory .. .. ,,		9 35	Boscombe .. .. .. ,,		10 53
Dover Marine .. .. ,,		9 45	Pokesdown .. .. .. ,,		10 56
Folkestone Central 10 7			Christchurch .. .. .. ,,		11 2
Margate Sands .. .. .. ,,		9B25	Brockenhurst .. .. .. ,,		11 22
Ramsgate Town .. .. .. ,,		9B38	Southampton West .. .. ,,		11 45
Sandwich .. .. ,,		8B48			p.m.
Canterbury West .. .. .. ,,		10B 0	Fareham .. .. ,,		12 14
Ashford (Kent) .. .. .. ,,		10 34	Havant .. .. ,,		12 32
Tunbridge Wells Central .. .. ,,		10C35	Petersfield .. .. ..arr.		12 57
Tonbridge .. .. ,,		11 10	Liss .. .. ,,		1 6
Red Hill .. .. ,,		11 40	Haslemere .. .. .. ,,		1 24
		p.m.	Godalming .. .. .. ,,		1 41
Guildford.. .. .. ..arr.		12 11	Guildford.. .. .. .. ,,		1 51

Week Days only.			Week Days only.		
Guildford.. .. .. ..dep.		12 33	Guildford.. .. .. ..dep.		1 56
Haslemere .. .. ,,		1 2	Red Hill .. ..arr.		2 30
Petersfield .. .. ,,		1 19	Tonbridge .. .. .. ,,		3F11
Southampton West .. ..arr.		2 18	Tunbridge Wells Central .. ,,		3F23
Brockenhurst .. .. .. ,,		2 43	Ashford (Kent).. .. .. ,,		3 29
Sway .. .. ,,		2 53	Canterbury West .. .. ,,		3B56
New Milton .. .. .. ,,		3 0	Ramsgate Town .. .. ,,		4B22
Hinton Admiral .. .. .. ,,		3 7	Margate Sands .. .. ,,		4B34
Christchurch .. .. .. ,,		3 14	Folkestone Central .. .. ,,		3 50
Pokesdown .. .. .. ,,		3 21	Dover Priory .. .. .. ,,		4 5
Boscombe .. .. .. ,,		3 24	Walmer .. .. ,,		4 25
Bournemouth { Central .. ,,		3 29	Deal .. .. ,,		4 30
{ West .. ,,		3 42	Sandwich .. .. .. ,,		5 40

TEA CAR. Guildford to Dover Marine.

B Change at Ashford.   C Change at Tonbridge.

F Change at Red Hill.

1924.

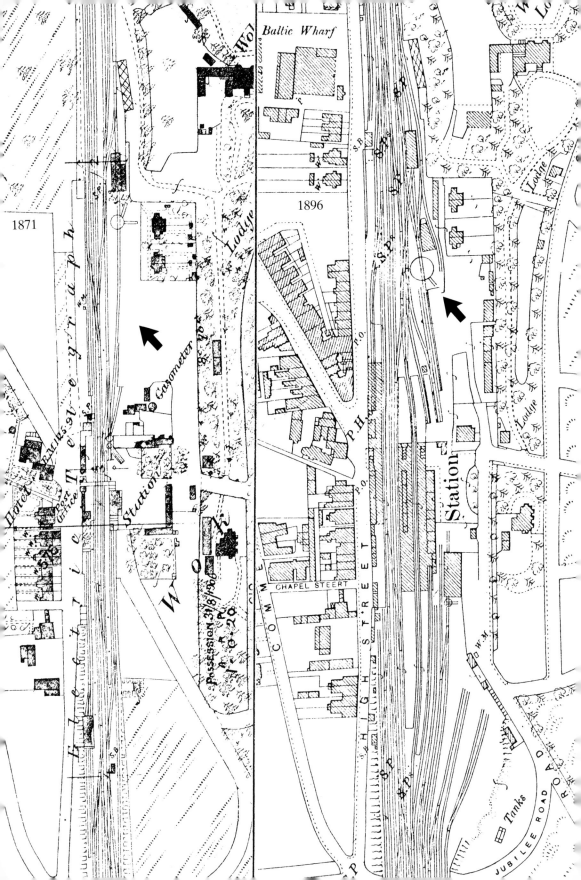

1871

1896

Baltic Wharf

Lodge

Lodge

CHAPEL STEERT

HIGH STREET

COOMBE

STATION

Station

Gasometer

Possession 31/8/1906

Tanks

JUBILEE ROAD

WOKING

1. For its first five years, the station was known as Woking Common, as Woking was 1½ miles distant. (This area is now called Old Woking). As the maps show, urban development close to the station was rather slow. This up train is headed by T3 class 4–4–0 no.570 whilst a slow train waits in the bay platform. (Lens of Sutton)

2. An up train hauled by class T9 no.704 passes the down junction signals whilst a ganger and his mate work on the up yard points and milk churns stand in the mid-day sun. They were presumably empties waiting for one of the westbound milk van trains run daily by the LSWR. (Lens of Sutton)

London and South Western Ry.

787

TO

LISS

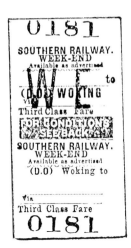

3. In the foreground is the up bay, uncluttered by passengers who might have produced a blur on the long exposure photographic plate. In the background, a railwayman appears to be securing a gun carriage onto a wagon. (Lens of Sutton)

4. The lady tending her car may be thinking that it is quicker by train whilst the London-bound passengers crowding the platform were probably wishing that they could afford a car. The bay platform (no. 1) has been lost in recent years to make way for a bus lay-by. (Lens of Sutton)

5. An eastward view from "Tin Bridges" shows the Guildford line on the right of the picture, the junction being largely obscured by the train departing for Basingstoke. The locomotive appers to be no.541, an 0–4–2 of class A12. (Lens of Sutton)

6. Great changes took place in 1937-38 – the introduction of electric traction; replacement of semaphore signals by colour lights and almost total rebuilding of the station in concrete. Here we see the new signal box under construcion. (D. Cullum collection)

7. Viewed in August 1950, the concrete luggage bridge and lift shafts still look new. The generous glazing of this bridge is in contrast to the unglazed footbridge behind. Maybe the drawings were transposed during their erection. The four-car corridor electric sets (4 COR) seen here were introduced for the fast services to Farnham and Portsmouth. The headcode stencil 8 indicates the latter destination. (J.H. Aston)

WOKING

8. Class 4 no. 76069 is seen with an engineer's train between the up yard and no. 2 platform, in the summer of 1966. The sky line has since changed, with the erection of multi-storey offices. (D. Fereday Glenn)

9. Unlike most goods yards, both up and down yards both still exist, although now used for permanent way materials. Another 1966 view shows two 2BILs on the first of many curves on the Portsmouth line whilst a class 33 Crompton shunts Esso tankers. The EMU and the locomotive were still in green livery. (J.A.M. Vaughan)

A restricted timetable was operated during the 1912 coal strike.

WOKING, GUILDFORD & PORTSMOUTH.   SUNDAYS.

	F	A.M.	A.M.	A.M.	P.M.	P.M.	E	P.M.	PM.	P.M.	PM.	P.M.	PM.	P.M.	PM.	A.M.	P.M.	PM.	P.M.	P.M.	P.M.	
Woking ... dep.	1 20	6 4	8 56	9 50	1239	1 53	2 16	3 36	4 30	...	6 0	7 18	8 17	9 38	1130	3 44	3 55	6 53	9 30	1137	...
Guildford ... ,,	1 30	6 20	9 10	10 6	1253	2 7	2 33	3 51	4 42	4 51	6 15	7 32	8 32	9 53	1145	9 59	10 7	9 9	44	1152	...
Farncombe arr.	STOP	6 26	9 16	1012	1259	2 13	2 39	3 57	...	4 57	6 21	7 38	8 38	9 59	1151	10 6	4 17	7 16	9 51	...	...
Godalming ,,		6 30	9 20	1016	1 3	2 17	2 43	4 1	...	5 1	6 25	7 42	8 42	10 9	1155	1010	4 21	7 21	9 54	12 2	...
Milford ...... ,,		6 37	9 27	1022	1 9	2 23	2 49	4 7	...	5 7	6 31	7 49	8 48	10 9	12 1	1016	4 27	7 27	STOP	12 9	...
Witley ...... ,,		6 44	9 34	1029	1 15	2 30	2 56	4 14	...	5 14	6 38	7 56	8 55	1016	12 8	1023	4 34	7 34		1216	...
Haslemere ,,		6 55	9 45	1040	1 26	2 41	3 7	4 25	5 6	5 25	6 49	8 7	9 6	1027	1219	1636	4 48	7 44		1228	...
Petersfield ,,		7 21	STOP	11 5	1 49	STOP	3 32	4 48	5 22	STOP	7 12	8 30	9 29	STOP	1213	11 3	5 13	STOP		1252	...
Portsmouth ,,		8 6		1148	2 31		STOP	5 30	6 0		7 56	STOP	1011		1 24	1146	STOP			1 28	...

10. An unusual sight just south of Woking on 30th April 1966 was *Gordon*, hauling an RCTS special composed of smartly turned out Bulleid-designed coaches. The locomotive was then in use on the Longmoor Military Railway and is now resident on the Severn Valley Railway. (S.C. Nash)

PORTSMOUTH TO GUILDFORD & WOKING.

	A.M.	A.M.	A.M.	A.M.	A.M.	A.M.	A.M.	A.M.	P.M.	E	P.M.	PM.	P.M.	P.M.	P.M	A.M.	P.M.	PM.	P.M.	P.M.	P.M.
Portsmouth dep.	...	...	...	6 53	...	...	8 55	1116	...	...	3 7	...	6 0	7 10	8 50	7 15	...	...	6 20	...	...
Petersfield ,,	...	...	7 5	7 42	...	...	9 38	1159	...	3 43	3 53	...	6 46	7 53	9 34	7 58	...	5 25	7 7	...	...
Haslemere ,,	6 28	7 20	7 46	8 11	...	9 48	1011	1231	2 55	4 11	4 27	6 10	7 21	8 25	10 6	8 33	...	5 54	7 42	8 10	...
Witley ...... ,,	6 37	7 29	7 58	8 20	...	9 57	1020	1240	3 4	4 20	4 36	6 20	7 31	8 35	1015	8 43	...	6 3	...	8 19	...
Milford ...... ,,	6 43	7 35	8 7	8 26	...	10 3	1026	1246	3 10	4 26	4 42	6 26	7 37	8 41	1021	8 49	...	6 9	...	8 26	...
Godalming ,,	6 49	7 40	8 15	8 31	...	10 8	1032	1252	3 15	4 31	4 48	6 31	7 43	8 47	1027	8 54	...	6 14	7 59	8 31	...
Farncombe ,,	6 53	7 44	8 22	8 35	...	1012	...	1257	3 19	4 35	4 52	6 35	7 47	8 51	1031	8 58	...	6 18	...	8 36	...
Guildford ... arr.	7 0	7 51	8 29	8 42	9 13	1019	1040	1 4	3 25	4 42	4 59	6 42	7 54	8 57	1038	9 5	2 15	6 25	8 7	8 43	9 40
Woking ...... ,,	7 15	8 6	8 47	8 54	9 22	1034	1053	1 20	3 40	5 0	5 17	6 58	8 11	9 13	1056	9 25	2 28	6 41	8 24	8 59	9 52

E Saturdays only.   **F** Not Mondays.

WORPLESDON

11. A typical SR country station – a partly sheeted wagon; a few boxes awaiting collection; a wagon loading gauge; co-acting starting signals and a signal box opposite a barrow crossing. Class M7 0–4–4T no.59 drifts in with a slow train to Waterloo on 10th July 1926. (H.C. Casserley)

1871

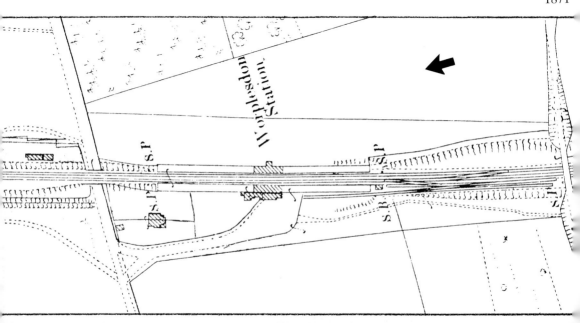

12. The footbridge from which the previous photograph was taken is still in use today. The parcels shed on the left now stores commuters' cycles and the goods yard has been transformed into the inevitable car park. (D. Cullum collection)

13. Most travellers on the line have not experienced the architectural variety and delights of the exterior of the station and its associated staff house. For many years it was the sixth successive station starting with W south of Walton. (V. Mitchell)

GUILDFORD

This 1870 map makes an interesting comparison with the 1916 edition reproduced in our *Branch Lines to Horsham*. The River Wey is marked with dashes.

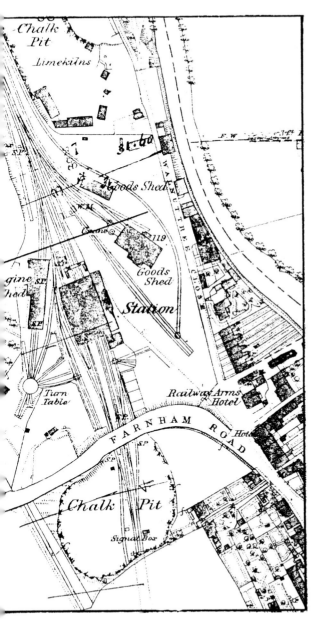

RAILWAY COMPENSATION.

TO THE EDITOR OF THE TIMES.

Sir,—About three years ago a lady, a cousin of mine, took a cottage close to Guildford, which she proceeded to furnish with a view towards lengthened residence. This cottage was substantially built, was surrounded by a nice flower garden, and stood on the last spur of the range of hills which overlook Guildford and the Godalming valley; in short, the situation was beautiful and the view lovely, as any of your readers acquainted with the neighbourhood of Guildford will understand, when I say that the cottage stood on the slope of the hill under the ruined Church of St. Katharine at Brabœuf.

Well, I went out of England, and in my absence often thought of my cousin and her charming cottage, and wished, as every true grumbling Englishman is sure to wish, that I were back in England, lying on my back in the garden at Guildford, smoking my weed (for this lady allowed that nasty practice out of doors), and admiring the view throughout the livelong summer day. Now, it has turned out in this, as in many like cases; I might have spared my longings for enjoyments which had no existence, except in my own imagination. Not very long ago I returned to Old England, and one of the first journeys I took was to Guildford to look after my cousin and her cottage. The hill on which it stands is not ten minutes' walk from the station " for a well-girded man," as Herodotus says, and with me the distance was accomplished in five, for I ran all the way. As I neared the hill and saw the cottage from a distance, it certainly struck me as looking wofully out of repair, and I reproached my cousin for stingyness in paint and whitewash, but it was not till I reached the gate that I could make up my mind that the building was what it is, a tumble-down ruin. The first surprise over, the cause of this destruction was soon explained. About the time I left England the South-Western Railway, in their zeal for extension, began to bore through that portion of St. Katharine's-hill which lies immediately under the cottage—a process which, if you will excuse the pun, proved such a great bore to my cousin that she speedily evacuated the place; indeed, if she had not done so, it would have tumbled about their ears, for it looks now for all the world like a house that has been mined and blown up. There it stands, torn, and rent, and shattered in every direction, almost every train that passes bringing down a bit, as I can testify from having been present when a train passed through the tunnel. Of course, it was no use looking for my cousin in the ruin; so, having ascertained her whereabout from some of the neighbours, and having smoked a weed in the desolate garden, and consoled myself with the lovely view, which still remained in spite of the railway, I returned to town, hugging myself at not being the tenant of a beautiful cottage on a hill under which a railway is extended, the more so as I was credibly informed that the company have, up to the present time, paid no compensation to the owner of this very cottage, who will, I suppose, have to trust for justice to the tender mercies of a jury. Under all the circumstances, it is rather lucky for the company that I am not likely to be one of the 12 men called on to assess the amount of damage in this case.

I am, Sir, your obedient servant,
SEMPER VIRENS.

From *The Times* of 11th March 1850.

14. The stations at both county towns of Sussex originally had roofs over the running lines, similar to this. In this northward view, circa 1870, it is evident that the water tank had two outlet pipes but only one was fitted with a bag for supplying locomotives.
(D. Cullum collection)

15. Viewed in the opposite direction, the Farnham Road bridge can be seen in the distance and the locomotive shed is on the right. The footbridge was erected in 1868.
(Guildford Museum)

BOROUGH OF GUILDFORD.

THE COMMITTEE OF MANAGEMENT of the GUILDFORD JUNCTION RAILWAY, having acquainted me that a Deputation from such Committee, assisted by MR. GILES, are desirous of conferring with the Inhabitants of this Borough on the subject of the proposed Terminus; I hereby convene a MEETING of the Inhabitants of the Borough for that purpose, to be held at the COUNCIL CHAMBER, on

WEDNESDAY NEXT, 7th OF FEB.,
At TWELVE o'Clock at Noon.

CASSTEELS COOPER,
Mayor.

Guildford, 3rd February, 1844.

[RUSSELLS, PRINTERS.]

16. The mayor and corporation together with the Rifle Volunteers prepare for an occasion which regrettably was not recorded on the photograph. Suggestions range from a royal visit to the opening of the railway to Horsham in 1865. (Guildford Museum)

17. The station was extensively rebuilt in the 1880s and largely survives in this form today, although giving the appearance of not having been touched since then. This is due to reconstruction plans having been deferred for various reasons for very many years. (Lens of Sutton)

18. On 16th February 1929, class L12 no.E425 emerges from the tunnel with a train from Portsmouth, the leading vehicle being a four-wheeled horse box. The signal sighting committee must have had problems with this signal. (H.C. Casserley)

19. The semi-roundhouse at Guildford always required a short wheelbase shed pilot engine. As a result there was always one unusual little locomotive to be seen there. In July 1939 it was this 21-ton Hawthorn Leslie saddle tank. (J.G. Sturt)

20. A rich variety of architectural features, pollarded trees and a fine porte cochere (under which the gentry alighted from their horse drawn carriages) all combine to create an imposing facade. The white patch on the front of the locally made Dennis bus was a legal requirement in the black-out of WWII. (British Rail)

21. Many will hope that some of the fine features of the present worn out station, such as this intricate drinking fountain, will be incorporated in the new station – eventually. (C. Hall)

22. The centenary of the opening of the line to Havant was marked with a commemorative train, hauled by a former LSWR goods engine, class 700 0–6–0 no.30350, with the crew wearing the uniform of the period. On the right is a class M7 0–4–4 tank. (A.E. Bennett)

23. The shed turntable was vacuum operated, the reinforced hose on the left being
simply connected to the locomotive's brake
pipe to obtain the necessary power. When
photographed in 1965, the shed pilot was
no.30072, an 0–6–0 tank built in the USA for
use in Europe during WWII. It is now preserved on the Keighley and Worth Valley
Railway. (J. Scrace)

24. Another special train was the LCGB
Sussex Coast Limited seen here rounding the
last curve on the Effingham Junction line on
24th June 1962. The class T9 locomotive had
been restored to LSWR livery and now forms
part of the Mid-Hants Railway fleet.
(A.E. Bennett)

25. In August 1965 construction was well advanced on a new panel box which would control all operations between Worplesdon and Farncombe. North Box is on the right. (British Rail)

26. With evidence of signalling and track remodelling visible, South Box did not have much life left when seen from under the steel span of Farnham Road bridge on 2nd February 1966. U class no.31791 is standing by the shed stores. (D. Fereday Glenn)

27. The dust from the coal stage and the smoke from the engines was not appreciated by passengers on platform 8. The class Q1 locomotive at the stage is no.33006. The footbridge in the background was erected in 1935. (D. Fereday Glenn)

28. A clear November day in 1984 shows (from left to right) the single line serving both platforms 6 and 7; the rear of the 13.46 Fridays only train for Leeds at platform 5; a class 47 at the head of the late running 06.45 departure from York standing at platform 4; an up train (4VEP) from Portsmouth arriving at platform 3 and a southbound stopping service about to leave from no.2.
(J.A.M. Vaughan)

29. Framed by one of the brick arches of the old part of Farnham Road bridge, we witness the first public working of the new replacement rolling stock for the Portsmouth line on 2nd June 1970. The units are nos.7338 and 7049, forming the 08.50 from Waterloo, complete with an inspection saloon. (J. Scrace)

30. At noon on 14th August 1954, a bridge collapsed onto the track between Chalk Tunnel (845 yds) and St. Catherine's Tunnel (132 yds). It had been scheduled for demolition and a temporary footbridge had been erected alongside it. Train services were suspended until 4pm, on one of the busiest Saturdays of the year, with 5000 passengers to be taken by bus around the blockage and many trains diverted. Look at the crumpled wheelbarrow. (British Rail)

31. An even more spectacular collapse had taken place on 23rd March 1895 in St. Catherine's Tunnel. This brick lined structure passes through fine sand, the bedding planes of which are almost vertical. In 1984 the tunnel was lengthened northwards, by means of concrete segments, to retain the unstable material. (Guildford Museum)

THE COLLAPSE OF ST. CATHERINE'S TUNNEL.

We publish to-day a view of the scene of the serious accident which took place on the London and South Western Railway last Saturday near Guildford. The view shows the exact spot where stood the coach-house, and stables occupied by Dr. Horace Wakefield. The coach-house and stables, with four carriages and two valuable horses, besides harness and all stable fittings and utensils, have disappeared into the tunnel. In addition to Dr. Wakefield's house there are a number of cottages in close proximity to the subsidence, and fears are entertained for their safety. An engine and part of a train of empty carriages are also buried. An engineer of the railway company considers that fully 1,000 tons of earth subsided into the tunnel, which is just below the scene illustrated.

RAILWAY ACCIDENT NEAR GUILDFORD.

Last week's news mentioned the frightful accident, between two and three o'clock on the Tuesday afternoon, to the express up train on the South-Western Railway from Portsmouth to London. It ran against a bullock, which had strayed from the neighbouring high road and had got on the line at Peasmarsh, between Godalming and Guildford. All the carriages were thrown off the rails. Some were overturned down an embankment and were crushed to pieces. Three persons—one a baby in its mother's arms—were killed instantly, and many others were injured. The engine and tender, breaking the chains by which they were coupled to the train, sprang over the body of the animal; and the engine, remaining on the rails, was enabled to run on to Guildford to convey news of the disaster. The station-master at Guildford, Mr. Dashper, acting with great promptitude, immediately sent a special train to render assistance. There were ten carriages in the overturned train; they rolled down the embankment, a height of eight or nine feet, into two adjacent fields. The destruction was terribly complete in two of the carriages—a first-class smoking-carriage, about the middle of the train, and a second-class carriage, the third from the engine. The wrecks of these two carriages, as they lay not long after the accident, are shown in our Illustrations, from photographs taken by the Surrey Photographic Company, of Guildford. It was in the second-class carriage that the effects were most fatal; as there Mrs. Henry Bridger, of Godalming, with her child, nine months old, and Miss Martin, daughter of the station-master at Milford, near Godalming, were killed. A man who sat next to these women escaped unhurt.

32. On 9th September 1873, a serious derailment took place south of the tunnels. It was fully described in the *Illustrated London News* the following week.
(Guildford Museum)

33. In addition to this LSWR signal box, the LBSCR provided their own box, a short way down the branch, where the single track commenced. This is shown in *Branch Lines to Horsham*, together with a map of Shalford Junction which also shows the route of the abortive connection to the SER.
(Late E. Wallis)

34. Looking north from the Portsmouth Road bridge on 27th February 1966, we see D815 hauling a Waterloo to Southampton Docks special, diverted due to electrification work on the direct route. The Horsham line, on the right, had closed the previous June.
(J. Scrace)

NGTON COLD
STORAGE

0' | 215' | 340'
0'   390'
       215

860'

PEASMARSH
Nº 2 SIDINGS

860'   360'

PEASMARSH
Nº 1 SIDING

620'   20'

PEASMARSH
JUNCTION

F.A.

F.A.

F.A.

(S)

TO BRAMLEY

F.A.

TO SHALFORD

FARNCOMBE

35. This station was opened on the same day that the original Godalming terminus was closed (1st May 1897) and served a developing residential area north of the River Wey. Here we look towards Guildford, with the junction signals to Godalming Old on the right. (Lens of Sutton)

36. The south elevation remains little altered today, as do most of the buildings. No goods yard was provided as the old terminus, half-way between Farncombe and Godalming (New) was retained for freight traffic. (Lens of Sutton)

37. West Box, visible in the distance, was provided with colour light signals in 1965 and lifting barriers in 1975. East Box was reduced from a block post to a gate box in 1934 and abolished in favour of CCTV cameras in 1975. The dock on the left of this 1937 view has been filled in. (National Railway Museum)

GODALMING OLD

1871 map showing the location of the goods and engine sheds.

38. The east elevation in 1937 shows the original passenger terminus in use as a goods office, a function it served until January 1969. The site was cleared for redevelopment in about 1972. (National Railway Museum)

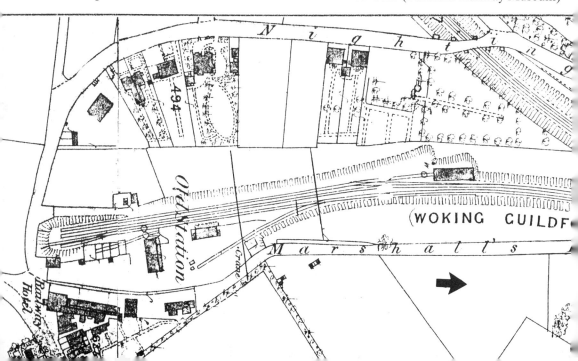

1897 map giving the position of the signal box (S.B.) and the additional goods sidings.

39. Looking north in 1937, we see the second goods shed and can compare the height of the original platform with its successor. A milk van body was later placed on the higher platform to act as an additional goods shed. (National Railway Museum)

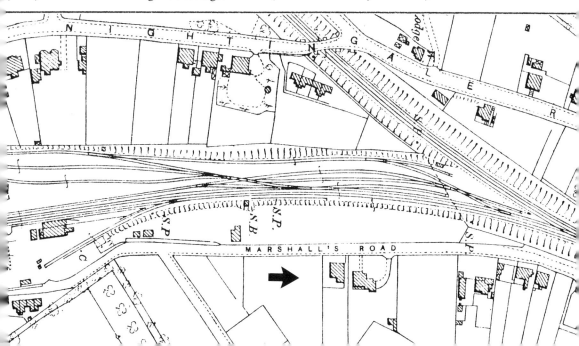

40. With Godalming Goods Junction in the background, David Shepherd's newly purchased class 9F passes on its way from Cricklewood to Longmoor on 7th April 1968. This impressive machine now operates on the East Somerset Railway. (S.C. Nash)

41. Class 5 MT 4–6–0 no.73115 stands at the approach to the goods yard on 1st April 1967, whilst 4COR set no.3135 heads an up fast from Portsmouth. The Wey Valley is in the background. (D. Fereday Glenn)

GODALMING NEW

42. In 1985 this fine facade was renovated as part of the first joint venture between BR and local industry in station conservation and redecoration. The beautiful stonework has been cleaned and the building repainted in the colours of Friary Meux, whose head office is now located nearby. (Lens of Sutton)

43. The up platform shelter has unfortunately been replaced by a characterless glass waiting room but the down platform retains its interesting outbuildings of various styles. The line crosses the River Wey just beyond the station. (Lens of Sutton)

The 1871 map confirms that the single line to Havant commenced at this station. Doubling was completed in 1878. A single dock siding similar to Farncombe's, is shown on what is now the site of the station's car park.

44. 1966 was the last Christmas that special parcel trains would be steam hauled. In 1967, steam was banished from the Southern Region. (D. Fereday Glenn)

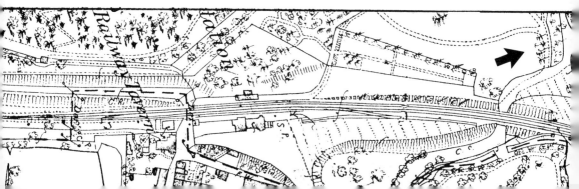

45. On the right of this 1967 photograph is the station master's office. On several other stations on the Southern, it was similarly located in a separate more peaceful building. The sharp curve through this station has always necessitated a speed restriction. (D. Cullum)

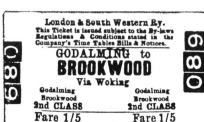

London & South Western Ry.
This Ticket is issued subject to the By-laws
Regulations & Conditions stated in the
Company's Time Tables Bills & Notices.
GODALMING to
BROOKWOOD
Via Woking
Godalming   Godalming
Brookwood   Brookwood
2nd CLASS   **2nd CLASS**
Fare 1/5   Fare 1/5
680   680

0024
SOUTHERN RAILWAY.
Issued subject to the Bye-laws,
Regulations & Conditions in the
Company's Bills and Notices.
Monthly as advertised.
Portsmouth & Southsea or
Portsmouth Harbour to
(584) **GUILDFORD**
Via Petersfield
First Class. Fare 15/11
NOT TRANSFERABLE.
SOUTHERN RAILWAY.
MONTHLY RETURN.
Guildford
Portsmouth & S'sea
or Portsmouth Har
584) Guildford to (584
PORTSMOUTH & S'SEA
or PORTSMOUTH HAR.
Via Petersfield
First Class. Fare 15/11
0024

SOUTHERN RAILWAY.
Issued subject to the Bye-laws, Regulations &
Conditions in the Company's Bills and Notices.
Available on DAY of issue ONLY.
Guildford to
HASLEMERE
THIRD CLASS
Issued in exchange for Return Ticket issued by
Aldershot & District Traction Coy. Ltd. upon
payment of supplementary charge of 7d.
NOT TRANSFERABLE.
0776   0776

MILFORD

46. An early postcard of indifferent quality is justified as it shows the up platform before the erection of the canopy. The station was the first passing place in the days of the single line. (Lens of Sutton)

1871 map

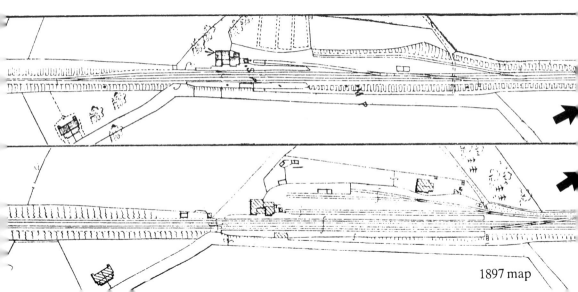

1897 map

47. The charming cottage style signal box was not unique on the line. Because of the acute angle between the road and the railway a special linkage was provided to partly rotate the gate lamp so that it was always correctly aligned to road or rail. (National Railway Museum)

48. Another 1937 photograph shows an up stopping train arriving. The remarkable unplanned roofscape is worthy of study. (National Railway Museum)

49. Hambledon R.D.C. had its own siding on the west side of the yard, by the shed in the distance. The station is nearly a mile from the village and so is one of the least busy on the line. (Lens of Sutton)

50. Evidence of retention of much of the brickwork of the earlier signal box is to be seen. The box was closed in December 1973 when automatic half barriers replaced the gates. The exterior of the station is unusual in that the only access to the booking office is from the platform. (J. Scrace)

WITLEY

51. With not a single female ankle to be seen, a London-bound train departs, displaying the shapely duckets of the guards van.

Although over a mile to Witley, the station also serves the equidistant villages of Hambledon and Brook. (Lens of Sutton)

→

1871 map. After doubling, an up siding and dock was added at the south end of the station.

53. This 1970 view shows the concrete ducts being positioned to receive cables for colour light signals. These rendered the signal box obsolete on 9th December 1973. The redundant goods shed aptly became the home of the Witley Model Railway Club. (J. Scrace)

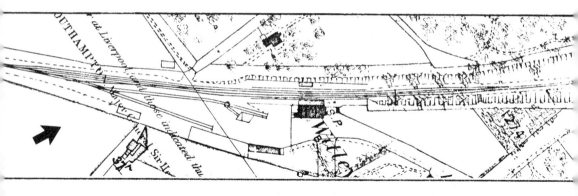

52. On 11th August 1937, U class 2–6–0 no. 1638 creates a good clear exhaust as she pounds up the incline with a heavy Reading to Portsmouth excursion. Since the previous photograph was taken, the glazing of the footbridge has been removed and the gas lanterns have become swan necks. (National Railway Museum)

54. The round-headed windows were typical of LSWR stations – the deep eaves were less so. Down draught seems to have been a problem with the chimneys and no doubt these could be the same problem in the well ventilated Gents. (J. Scrace)

55. London season ticket holders have proliferated since electrification brought a much improved service. Another traffic that might have developed is oil. A deep well was sunk nearby in 1983 but it produced gas instead. (C. Hall)

56. South of Witley, the line crosses Wealden clay which gives an unstable base to the embankments. This slip took place in February 1904. It has happened many times since, notably in 1946 and 1968. (British Rail)

HASLEMERE

57. In the mid-1920s, the station became the focus of a number of rural bus routes. The places mentioned on these solid-tyred Daimlers were soon linked by route 19 (now 219). Behind them is the now familiar architectural style. (Haslemere Museum)

The 1871 map reveals no urban development in the vicinity of the station, the centre of the small town being ½ mile distant.

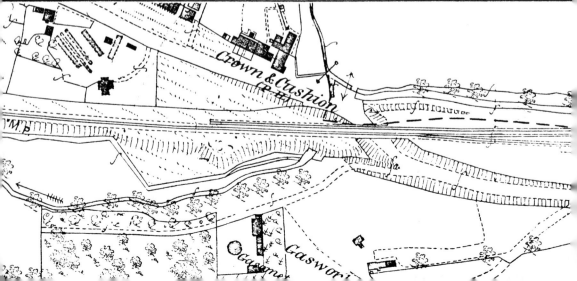

58. The Schools class 4–4–0s were built in 1930-35 and were a great success on the difficult gradients of the Portsmouth Direct line. Here no.925 *Cheltenham* arrives with a down train, passing the up starting signal. Unfortunately the top arm of the co-acting signals is off the picture. It was necessary because the footbridge obscured the view of the lower one, when approaching the station. (H.C. Casserley)

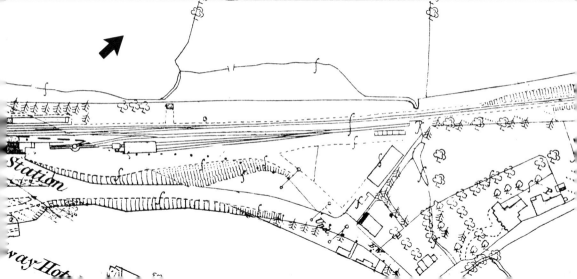

59. Another Schools class, *Kings Canterbury*, is seen bound for Portsmouth, only six weeks before electric services began. The signal box remains in use today, controlling colour light signals entirely. (National Railway Museum)

61. Amidst six electric trains per hour, a steam-hauled passenger train was very photogenic. After rebuilding from their streamlined form, the aesthetics of the West Country class were generally thought to have been improved. This example is *Clovelly* and is hauling a Portsmouth Harbour to Colne relief train. (S.C. Nash) ⟶

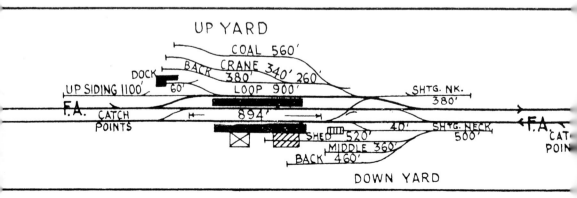

UP YARD

COAL 560'

CRANE 340' 260'

BACK 380'

DOCK 60'

LOOP 900'

UP SIDING 1100'

SHTG. NK. 380'

F.A. CATCH POINTS

894'

SHTG. NECK 500'

F.A. CAT POIN

SHED 520' 40'

MIDDLE 360'

BACK 460'

DOWN YARD

50. A pick-up goods stands in the up loop on 4th August 1961, when the platforms were still gas lit. A banner repeater signal had been installed to overcome the problem of "sighting the starter". (D. Cullum)

62. No.2 platform is signalled for reversible running so that a down train can be held there to allow another to pass, such as the down Manchester express. On 7th July 1984, an elderly ex-Metropolitan locomotive *Sarah Siddons* is resting there with a special train to Portsmouth. (J. Scrace)

63. Half a mile west of the station, a footpath is carried over the line by this unusual construction. Sickle Mill bridge was photographed in 1903, together with the inevitable children who appeared whenever a camera was erected. (British Rail)

LIPHOOK

Railway Station, Liphook.

64. A faded Edwardian postcard reveals the goods yard beyond the road bridge and a dip in the platforms at the foot crossing, necessary prior to the erection of a footbridge. (Lens of Sutton)

A 6″ to the mile map showing the remoteness of the station from the village in the 1870s.

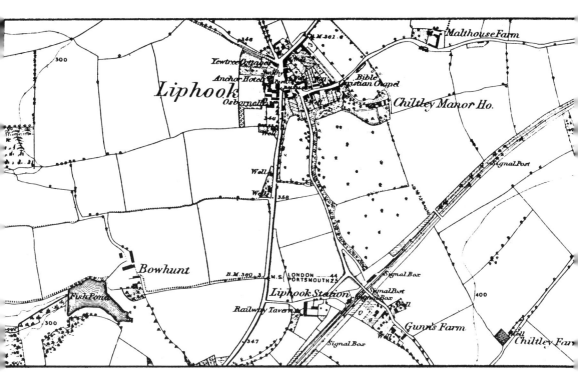

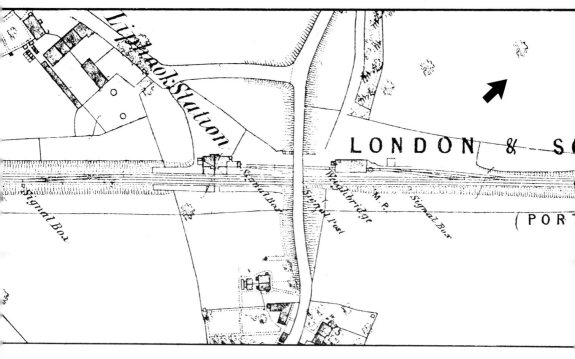

65. Drummond designed class D15 4–4–0 no.467 is approaching with an up train on 21st March 1936. Observe a complete LSWR coacting signal; an SR upper quadrant signal and a vintage caravan. (H.C. Casserley)

The 1870 map, showing two signal boxes.

66. Another D15 ambles in with an assortment of coaches, just prior to electrification and when ankles could be exposed to view. (National Railway Museum)

67. This 1961 view reveals the goods yard gate on the left and the pleasing symmetry of this series of country stations. One hopes that these important features of local history can be preserved, maybe with more sponsorship from industry or commerce. (D. Cullum)

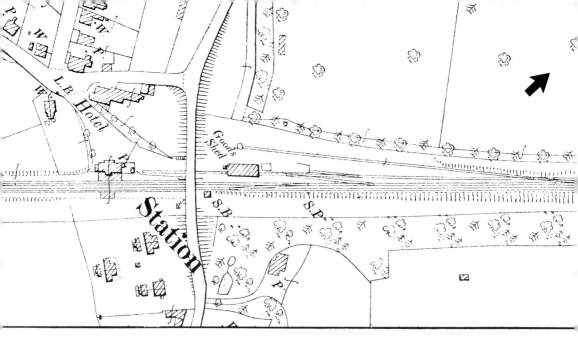

1896.

68. Class 4VEP no.7777 on a down stopping train in September 1969, approaches the signal box which was subsequently moved one mile south east, to be preserved with the Hollycombe Steam Collection. Behind the goods yard there had been a siding over 500 yards long, serving Army stores. (J. Scrace)

70. After crossing the watershed between the Rivers Wey and Rother at Weavers Down, southbound travellers reach Liss Common, ½ mile before Liss station. It is now the only crossing in this section and was fitted with half barriers in December 1967.

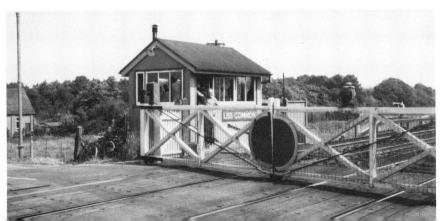

71. A postcard view looking north shows the goods shed in the distance. The main buildings on the down side were demolished by BR due to severe settlement. They have been replaced by a steel and glass structure but the old up platform shelter remains in use. (Lens of Sutton)

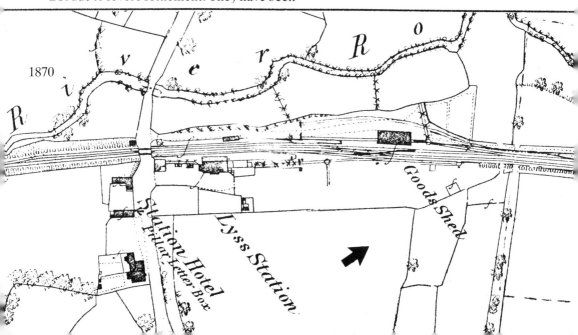

72. Another postcard gives an impression of the commercial development that eventually took place in Station Road. To the left of the signal box is *Station Hotel*, renamed *The Crossing Gates*. (G. Knight collection)

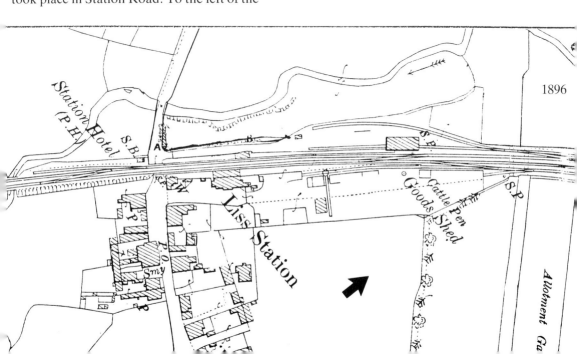

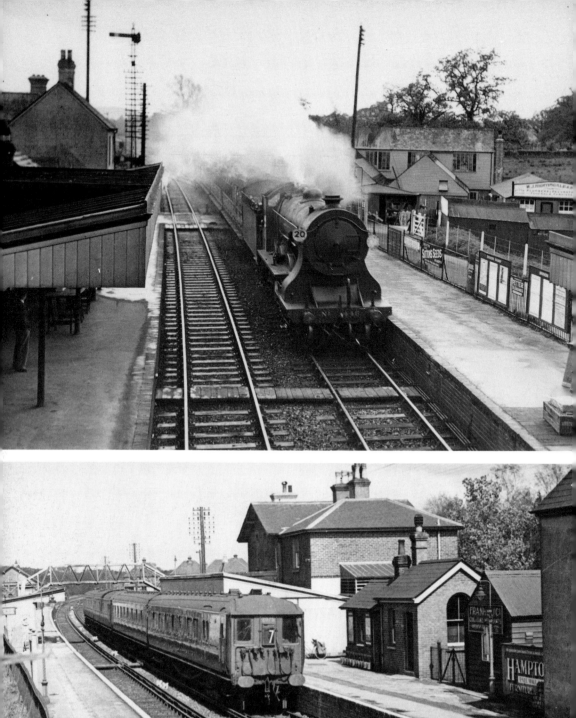

73. One of the "Paddlebox" 4–6–0s, no.446 of class T14, runs in with an up train on 17th May 1934. The sheds on the right were small shops and stood on ground that was to become the terminus of the Longmoor Military Railway. (H.C. Casserley)

74. 2BILs operated the half-hourly stopping trains for over 30 years. Here two such units stand in the down platform in the last summer before WWII. The gas light controls can be studied in the foreground. (National Railway Museum)

75. Class N 2–6–0 no.311401 struggles to maintain the momentum of its heavy freight train, as it starts the two mile climb at 1 in 80 towards Liphook on 7th January 1961. (S.C. Nash)

76. From the same spot on the same day, we see no.34020 *Seaton* racing down the incline with a Peterborough to Portsmouth excursion. The signal post is of the typical LSWR lattice construction – lightweight but prone to rust. (S.C. Nash)

78. The LMR officially closed on 31st October 1969. A number of privately owned locomotives had been stored at Longmoor for about two years and, following an agreement between the Army and the ARPS on 30th April 1970, they were moved to Liss and fenced in. Occasional trips were made to Liss Forest but residents objected to their permanent presence and they were dispersed, before the BR connection was lifted on 31st October 1971. The Army's *Gordon* is sheeted up; next to it is David Shepherd's class 9F and beyond is his class 4MT no.75029. (D. Meek)

77. The Longmoor Military Railway was extended southwards to Liss in August 1933 but was only connected to the SR at Bordon until 18th April 1943, when exchange sidings were brought into use at Liss. Soon five trains per day plus 200 wagons per month were transferred here. LMR no.195 blows off at the terminus on 1st June 1967. This platform was adjacent to the BR up platform.
(D. Fereday Glenn)

4–6–2	34023	**Blackmore Vale**
4–6–2	35028	**Clan Line**
2–10–0	600	**Gordon**
2–10–0	92203	**Black Prince**
4–6–0	75029	**The Green Knight**
0–6–0ST	188	**(ex-Army)**
0–6–0T	30064	**(USA tank)**
0–4–0T	30096	**Corrall Queen**

The stored locomotives and rolling stock were open to the public from June 1970 at weekends – admission 2/- (10p).

79. The signal box had 22 levers but did not directly control entry into the military exchange sidings, this being delegated to a ground frame at the other end of the station. When photographed in 1969, the 300yd long up siding beyond the crossing was still in use, as were gas lights on the station. (J. Scrace)

80. The line follows the River Rother closely for two miles south of Liss. It is a nearby bridge over this river that gives its name to this level crossing. The gates were replaced by automatic half barriers on 10th July 1967. Beside the dustbin is a can for drinking water, the bucket caught rainwater for other purposes. (D. Cullum)

PRINCES BRIDGE

81. Sheet crossing looking towards Stodham crossing and Liss in March 1966. AHBs took over here in February 1967. (D. Cullum)

82. The fourth crossing between Liss and Petersfield was Kings Fernsden, which was similarly modernised in September 1966. Unlike the other three, the building was on the up side. (D. Cullum)

83. This 1911 photograph reveals that the station was still gas lit and provided with locomotive water columns. As the maps show, there was also a locomotive turntable as there were for many years several trains each day that terminated here. (British Rail)

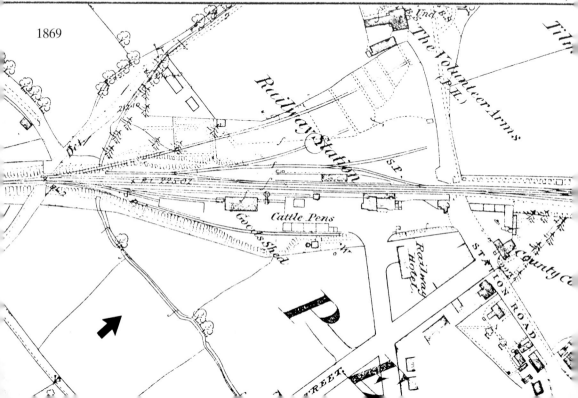

1869

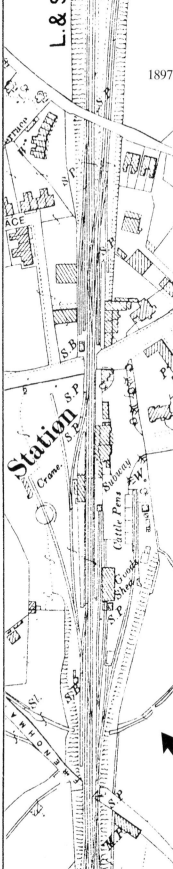

84. The view from the footbridge in 1911 is little altered today. The signals were modernised in 1969; the goods shed demolished and the loop line converted to an engineer's siding. (British Rail)

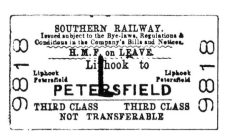

SOUTHERN RAILWAY.
Issued subject to the Bye-laws, Regulations &
Conditions in the Company's Bills and Notices.
H.M.F. on LEAVE
Liphook to
Liphook   Liphook
Petersfield   Petersfield
PETERSFIELD
THIRD CLASS   THIRD CLASS
NOT TRANSFERABLE
9818   9818

SOUTHERN RAILWAY.
This Ticket is issued subject to the By-laws
Regulations & Conditions stated in the
Company's Time-Tables Bills & Notices
HASLEMERE to
PETERSFIELD
Haslemere   Haslemere
Petersfield   Petersfield
3rd CLASS   3rd CLASS
Fare 1/6   Fare 1/6
7722   7722

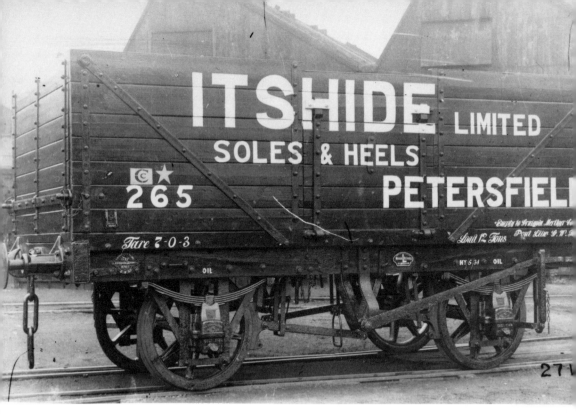

85. Itshide was in fact a light-coloured rubber for footwear and not hide. The ITS Rubber Co. had their own siding parallel to the Midhurst branch. ITS were the initial letters of the founders – Ingwer Tufford & Smith. Their wagon was photographed after being refurbished in Birmingham. (HMRS)

86. Class X2 no.588 pauses at Petersfield on 30th August 1930, with roof boards on the coaches and a choice of couplings on the drawbar. (H.C. Casserley)

87. Another view from the footbridge shows a push-pull train arriving from Midhurst at the separate branch platform, which was built sometime between the dates of the two maps. It was inconvenient for passengers, with only one seat and no shelter but kept the main lines clear, except if there was a heavy box of fish or a trunk destined for the branch. The train would then be shunted into the main station to minimise labour. A wagon stands in the SE Farmer's siding, beside the dairy. (Lens of Sutton)

88. Lord Nelson class no.30856 *Lord St. Vincent* heads south with an enthusiasts' special on 30th April 1961. The flat roofed building on the right houses a ground frame that replaced the South Box in 1902. The down yard closed in 1967 and the up yard two years later. (S.C. Nash)

89. The signal box survives today, controlling full barriers, installed in 1973. Beyond the box in this 1967 view is the former SCATS dock. Details of the sidings are shown in the diagram, and other photographs and maps are to be found in our *Branch Lines to Midhurst*. (J. Scrace)

90. An unusual visitor on 1st May 1983 was this retired suburban unit, 4SUB 4732, restored to its original Southern green livery, apart from the modern yellow ends. All regular electric services had toilet facilities. (C. Wilson)

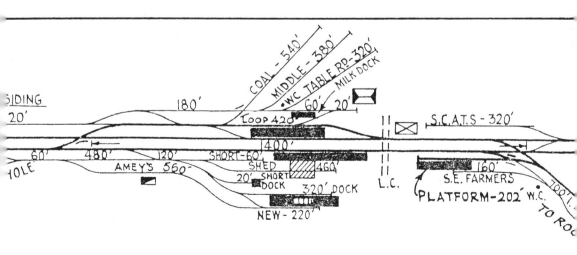

91. The design is basically the same as the other important station on the line – Godalming (Haslemere was a late developer). The stucco is less appealing than natural stone but the chimney stacks hint that the whole building may be stone built also. (V. Mitchell)

1924

PORTSMOUTH, HAVANT, PETERSFIELD, and LONDON.—Southern.

Week Days.

	Up.																								
	Ryde Pier * ...dep.																							
	Portsmouth Har... "																							
1	" & Southsea "																							
1½	Fratton																							
5	Havant 239																							
11½	Rowland's Castle																							
19½	Petersfield 178 {arr. / dep.																							
23	Liss																							
27½	Liphook																							
31½	Haslemere																							
36	Witley †																							
38	Milford																							
40	Godalming																							
41	Farncombe ..[225, 272																							
44	Guildford 185, 194, arr.																							
50	Woking ‡ 148, 175 "																							
55½	Weybridge "																							
62½	Surbiton 180 "																							
74¼	WATERLOO 172 "																							

Week Days—Continued. / **Sundays.**

Up.		
Ryde Pier * ...dep.		
Portsmouth Harbour.. "		
" and Southsea "		
Fratton		
Havant 239		
Rowland's Castle		
Petersfield 178 {arr. / dep.		
Liss		
Liphook		
Haslemere		
Witley, for Chiddingfold "		
Milford		
Godalming		
Farncombe ......[225, 272		
Guildford 185, 194, arr.		
Woking ‡ 148, 175 .. "		
Weybridge "		
Surbiton 180 ...... "		
WATERLOO 172 ...... "		

NOTES.

☞ For Local Trains and intermediate Stations

	BETWEEN	PAGE
Waterloo and Surbiton		180, 185, 188
Waterloo and Woking		180
Waterloo & Guildford		180, 155

✷✶✷ For other Trains

		PAGE
London and Portsmouth		210
Havant & Portsmouth 210, 216		
Fratton and Portsmouth Harbour		170

A Leaves at 7 aft. on Saturdays. **A** Runs on alternate Wednesdays only (Petersfield Market Days). **b** Restaurant Car. **c** Light Refreshments served. **d** Through Train from Bournemouth West (dep. 10 35 mrn.); also Through Carriages for Dover will be attached, see pages 159, 170, 273, 274, and 251. **D** Dining Car. **E** Except Saturdays. **F** Runs 9 minutes later on Saturdays. **S** Saturdays only. ***** By Boat. **†** Station for Chiddingfold. **‡** Station for Cobham (3½ miles). To Woking Village (1½ miles). **§** Station for Brooklands, St. George's Hill, and Oaklands Park. ****** Portsmouth and Southsea.

BURITON SIDING

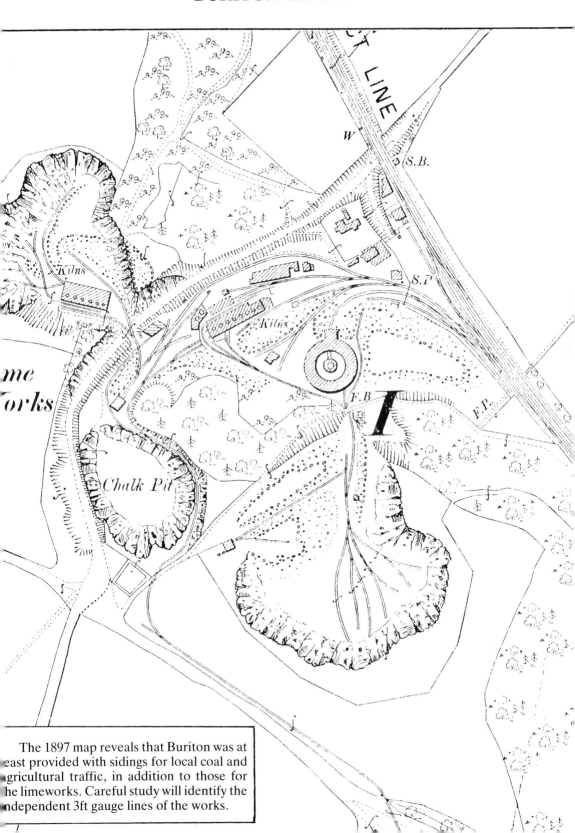

The 1897 map reveals that Buriton was at least provided with sidings for local coal and agricultural traffic, in addition to those for the limeworks. Careful study will identify the independent 3ft gauge lines of the works.

92. This Downs foot village was for centuries of greater importance than Petersfield. The villagers have, more than once, petitioned for a station to be built but the gradient of 1 in 110 is too steep for one to be approved. Southbound Schools class *Radley* climbs between the two overbridges on 21st March 1936. (H.C. Casserley)

93. No.34093 *Saunton* passes the solitary remaining siding on 27th February 1966, hauling the down Bournemouth Belle, diverted from its normal route due to engineering works. (J. Scrace)

94. The cottage-style box was similar to Milford's and was closed on 11th January 1970. Surplus colour light signals were acquired by the Ffestiniog Railway for use at their new passing loop at Rhiw Goch. (J. Scrace)

95. Owing to its low level, few passengers realised that a staff halt existed at the north end of the 485yd tunnel but permanent way staff alighting from the last train one night, found that two sailors had also detrained at this dark remote location. The structure was demolished shortly after being photographed in April 1983. (V. Mitchell)

96. This was situated about 5 miles from Petersfield and 3 from Rowlands Castle, near the remote hamlet of Chalton. The unlit platforms were in use from 26th August 1943 until 23rd July 1945 for Naval personnel visiting a hostel established in Ditcham House. In 1944 there was a down departure at 7.14am daily and an up service at 5.00pm (2.50pm Saturdays and 9.24am Sundays). The nearby topiary was photographed at 1/1000 of a second on 16th February 1985 and can be seen from the Chalton road bridge. It was created from a yew bush in the hedge in the mid-1930s by some permanent way workers. Mr. Arthur Hall can remember training it initially with wire. Another local resident, Mr. John Cole, has recollections of a siding, on the down about a mile north of the footbridge, being in use in 1927 for the despatch of timber from a nearby sawmill. (V. Mitchell)

97. This faded picture is interesting because it is so early. One clue to its date is the lever and rodding of a hand-worked point in the running line in the foreground, there being no interlocking. Where the awning meets the main building there is the white post of the station signal which was not a semaphore but a disc. It is so high that it is out of the picture, but could be seen from a great distance, which was vital when trains had only hand brakes. (Mrs. D. Rubick collection)

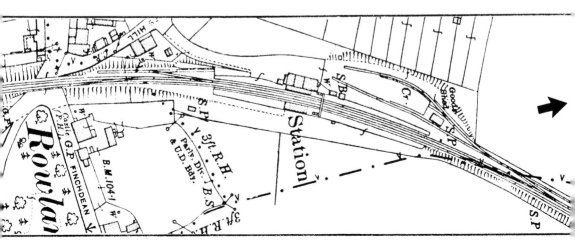

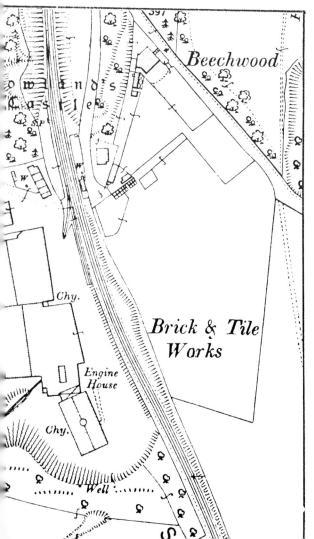

98. In March 1936, oil lamps and lower quadrant signal persisted in use, as a south-bound class D15 4–4–0 takes the sharp curve, which presently has a speed limit of 50mph. (H.C. Casserley)

This map is of the brickworks just south of the station, as surveyed in 1932. The 2ft gauge lines were in use until about 1952 and the standard gauge sidings until 1964. The latter could hold 17 wagons.

99. The most southerly of the standardised stations on the line was photographed in 1937. Beyond the barrow loaded with soap is the signal box and the goods shed. (National Railway Museum)

100. A standard SR concrete footbridge, made at their Exmouth Junction Works, replaced the earlier wooden structure. At the north end of the station on 10th August 1976, part of an engineer's train ran away under gravity and collided with the other half. The mess van was destroyed in the resulting smash. A third disaster occurred the following day when a 75-ton capacity crane toppled over whilst lifting a van. (J. Scrace)

101. The goods yard closed in 1961 but the signal box remained in use until 1970. The small shed on the left was for goods carried by passenger train. This was a quicker but more expensive service. (J. Scrace)

102. The Earl of Bessborough required the sharp curves to be made in the railway's alignment (to minimise its impact on his Stansted Park); two road bridges to be built (when one would be adequate) and ordered that they be finished with these ornate flint panels. An earlier Lord Bessborough exercised his right to stop trains for his use when it pleased him, but the present Lord drives to Havant. (V. Mitchell)

HAVANT

03. Site of the Battle of Havant. A fast train from Waterloo is reduced to 30mph at the unction as it passes the siding that once erved the warehouse of SCATS – the Southrn Counties Agricultural Trading Society.

Maps and other photographs of this station appear in our *Branch Line to Hayling* and *South Coast Railways – Chichester to Portsmouth*. (C. Wilson)

104. A 1936 photograph shows ex-LSWR signals on the up platform but LBSCR pattern still in use on the branch to Hayling, seen on the right of the picture. On the left is ex-LBSCR class E4 0–6–2T no.2562 and in the centre is ex-LSWR class 700 0–6–0 no.692. (H.C. Casserley)

L. B. & S. C. RY.

Available on the **DATE** of issue **ONLY**.
This ticket is issued subject to the Regulations
& Conditions stated in the Company's Time
Tables & Bills.

CHICHESTER

TO

HAVANT ha

THIRD CLASS.

1/4 Revised Fare. 1/4

8442 8442

106. The King Arthur class was principally employed on passenger services but here we witness *Sir Durnore* on an up van train to Guildford on 7th January 1961. The washing hanging in the gardens would be white for only another minute. (S.C. Nash)

105. A local train (probably the "Chichester Motor") stands in the up platform on 2nd October 1937, shortly before major reconstruction of the station commenced. This also involved quadrupling the track, lengthening the platforms considerably and abolishing the level crossing, visible in the distance. On the left is the bay platform for Hayling Island trains. (H.C. Casserley)

107. A point in the level crossing gave rise to some complicated timberwork – the shunting neck across it gave rise to some long delays to road users. This March 1966 view shows buses standing on the site of the Hayling bay; an ambulance from a local body builder ready for despatch on a flat wagon and a Blackpool tramcar ready for use on the Hayling line. Preservation of the branch did come about but a fresh revival scheme was launched in 1985. (D. Cullum)

BEDHAMPTON

109. Bedhampton Halt was one of a number of halts opened on 1st April 1906 and was served by the Portsmouth - Chichester Motor Train. The platforms have been progressively lengthened, taking six cars by 25th April 1965 when this up boat train from Southampton passed through.
(E. Wilmshurst)

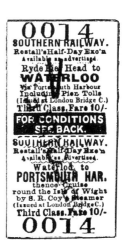

108. No.33017 hauls a special royal train on 6th December 1974. It left Waterloo at 09.35, bound for Southampton. The centre roads are little used nowadays and maybe abolished, although the up through line in mid-winter often accommodates a diesel locomotive used for banking electric trains over the hills to Guildford. (J. Scrace)

HILSEA

PORTSMOUTH, MIDHURST, PETERSFIELD, GUILDFORD, and LONDON.—London and South Western.

Up. — Week Days.

Miles	Up.	mrn	mrn	mrn	mrn	mrn	mrn	mrn	mrn	mrn	mrn	mrn	mrn	aft	aft	aft	aft	aft	aft	aft	aft	aft	aft	aft	aft	aft
	Ryde (per Boat) ....dep.						7 c 5		8 0	8 57			1010	1115				2 0			2 0					5
	Portsmouth Harbour....			7 10	7c40			8 50	9 35		10 8		110	12 0			2 45			3 0					5 4
	" Town			7 15	7 55			8 55	9 41		1014	1035	116	12 6	1 15		2 51			3 7					5 3
	167 Southsea (East) m dep.			7 19	8 0			8 59	9 45		1018	1038	1120	1211	1 18		2 56			3 11					5 3
14	Fratton and Southsea 167									9 50	1019		110	1150	1250		2 30			3 11					5 3
8	Havant 184			7 31				9 11	9 57		1030	1050	1132	1224	1 30		3 24								6
114	Rowland's Castle			7 36				9 19			1038	112	1140		1 38		3 33								
194	Petersfield 138 .... arr.			7 55				9 35	1017		1054	1119	1156	1245	1 54		3 49								6
—	Mls Midhurst ....dep			7 18				8 45	9 48				1218				3 10	4 35							5
—	3 Elsted			7 25				8 52	9 55				1225				3 17	4 42							5
—	5 Rogate and Harting			7 36				8 57	10 0				1230				3 22	4 47							6
—	94 Petersfield 138 .. arr.			7 45				9 6	10 9				1239				3 31	4 56							6
—	Petersfield ....dep.			7 59		8 39		9 38	1019	1057		1159	1248	1257		2 25			3 52						6
23	Liss				8 7	8 47		9 47		11 5		128	1 5		2 33				4 1						
274	Liphook				8 19			10 0		1117		1217	1 18		2 44				4 14						
314	Haslemere	6 28	7 20	7 51	8 28	8 48	9 10		9 43	1011		1127	1229		2 54			4 3	4 25		5 25			
36	Witley and Chiddingfold.	6 38	7 29	8 38	37		9 18		9 57	1020		1137	1238	1 37	3 3			4 12	4 34		5 34		6 20	
38	Milford	6 43	7 34	8 11	8 42		9 23		10 2	1025		1142	1243	1 42	3 8			4 17	4 39		5 39		6 25	
40	Godalming	6 50	7 40	8 18	8 48		9 29	9 48	10 8	1032		1148	1250	123	1 48	2 45	3 14		4 23	4 46		5 45	6 31	
41	Farncombe	6 54	7 44	8 22	8 52		9 33	9 52	1012			1152		1 52	2 49	3 18		4 27	4 50		5 48	6 35	
44	Guildford 155, 156, { arr.	7 1	7 51	8 29	8 59	9 7	9 40	9 59	1019	1040	1055		1255	1 57	2 49	3 18		4 34	4 57		5 55	6 42	
	194, 248 { dep.	6 15	7 3	7 53	8 49		9 12	9 43	10 3	1029	1042	1057	11 5	12 4	1 59		2 56	3 25	3 59		4 34	4 57	5 29	6
474	Worplesdon		7 10	8 1	8 46			9 50				115	12 4		2 12			3 37	4 32			5 36	6 16	
50	Woking ¶ 120, 148, 156.	6 25	7 18	8 8	8 53			9 55	1014		1053		1117	1217		1 21		2 17		3 42		4 37	4 48	5 10
624	Surbiton 150, 154	7 52							1051	1120			1246			1 54		3 5		3 51	4 35		5 85	42
704	Clapham Junction * 118.				9635								1259			2 12		3 26		4 8	4 54		5 21	6
73	Vauxhall		8 10		9 41		9 48		11 9	1137	1126	1132		1 5		2 19	2 16	3 34		4 14	5 0		5 28	6
744	WATERLOO ¶ 401 .... arr.		8 17	8 46	9 48		9 55	1041	1117	1144	1133	1139		1 12		2 26	2 23	3 42		4 21	5 7	4 48	5 35	6

Up. — Week Days—(continued). | Sundays. | NOTES.

Up.	aft	aft	aft	aft	afu	mrn	mrn	mrn	aft	aft	aft	aft	aft	aft	aft
Ryde (per Boat) ....dep.	6 18	6 18							5 5						
Portsmouth Harbour....	7 0	7 0							6 40						
" Town	7 6	7 6		8 50	11 0		7 15		6 48		8 45				
167 Southsea (East) m dep.	6 50	6 50		7 30											
Fratton and Southsea 167	7 10	7 14		8 55	11 3		7 18		6 52		8 49				
Havant 184		7 26		9 7	1115		7 30		7 5		9 2				
Rowland's Castle		7 34		9 15	1123		7 38		7 14		9 10				
Petersfield 138 .... arr.	7 39	7 50		9 31	1139		7 54		7 30		9 26				
Midhurst ....dep.	7 12			8 40			7 18	1020	6 40						
Elsted	7 19			8 47			7 28	1027	6 50						
Rogate and Harting	7 24			8 52			7 36	1032	6 59						
Petersfield 138 .... arr.	7 33			9 1			7 45	1041	7 10						
Petersfield ....dep.	7 40	7 53	8 45	9 34	1141		7 57		7 35		9 29				
Liss		8 2	8 53	9 43	1149		8 8		7 46		9 37				
Liphook		8 15	9 4	9 55	1159		8 22		7 59		9 49				
Haslemere		8 25	9 14	10 4			8 32		4 44	7 50	8 10	9 59			
Witley and Chiddingfold.		8 35	9 23	1013			8 41		4 53	7 59	8 19	10 8			
Milford		8 40	9 28	1018			8 47		4 58	8 4	8 25	1013			
Godalming		8 47	9 34	1025			8 53	12 55	4	8 9	8 31	1020	1030		
Farncombe		8 51	9 38	1029			8 57	12 95	8	8 12	8 35	9 39	1024	1034	
Guildford 155, 156, { arr.	8 16	8 55	9 45	1036			9 4	1216	5 15	8	19	8 42	9 46	1031	1041
194, 248 { dep.	8 19	9 0	9 49	1040		8 24	9 8	1218	5	176	55	23	8 47	9 49	1034
Worplesdon		9 8	9 56	1048		8 29	9 15	1225	5	05	7	38	30		9 57	1042
Woking ¶ 120, 148, 156.	8 28	9 13	10 1	1053		8 39	9 20	1232	5	30	7 9	8	37	8 57	10 3	1047
Surbiton 150, 154	8 44	9 41				9 15	9 55		1 12	6	07	459	16 9	2	1037	1114
Clapham Junction * 118.		9 56	1048			9 32	1017		1 34	6	178	39	389	46	1054	1131
Vauxhall	8 59	10 3	1055	1152		9 39	1026		1 41	6	238	109	439	51	11 0	1138
WATERLOO ¶ 401 .... arr.	9 6	1010	11 2	1159		9 46	1035		1 48	6	318	179	51	10 3	11 7	1145

NOTES.

a Stop to take up.
b Stop to set down.
c Mondays only.
m Motor Car, 1st and 3rd cl
* Mid Battersea, 1¼ miles ... Clapham.

¶ For Local Trai[ns] and intermediate static[ons] BETWEEN London and Woking ... 150 to

For other Tr[ains] BETWEEN London and Guildford ... 248 to Havant and Portsmouth ... 184 to Fratton and Portsmou[th] Harbour 140

110. Opened as Hilsea Halt on 2nd November 1941, as a war-time emergency measure, it facilitated transport of workers to nearby factories. This southward view shows the long-lost Hilsea gasholders in the distance. (D. Cullum)

111. The coal gasworks was replaced in the mid-1960s by one producing methane from naphtha, a low grade petrol. It is no longer available as a by-product and so the plant is redundant. The last train of tankers is seen leaving behind class 33 *Ashford* on September 18th 1985, removing the residual feedstock from the last rail connected gas premises in the South of England. (Southern Gas)

Bradshaw 1910

FRATTON

112. For over 30 years after the railway arrived, the Fratton area was largely agricultural. The station was not opened until 1st July 1885, when the East Southsea branch came into use. The branch platforms are in the background of this southward view. (Lens of Sutton)

113. A 12-coach fast train from Waterloo runs non-stop through the down loop on 28th July 1979, whilst the locomotive of a Bristol or Cardiff train stands in the fuelling road. Since the abolition of DMUs on services to these cities, regular light engine running from here to Harbour station is necessary between trains. (J. Scrace)

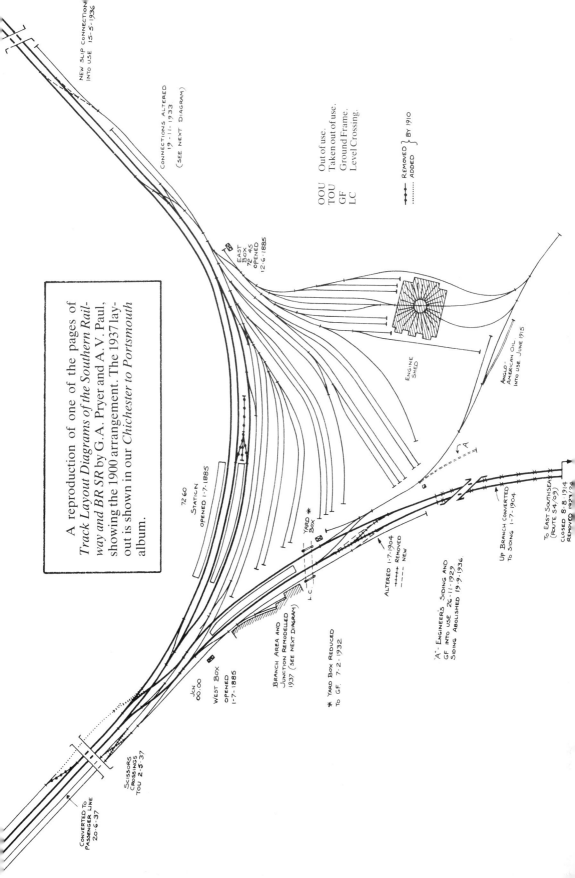

A reproduction of one of the pages of *Track Layout Diagrams of the Southern Railway and BR SR* by G.A. Pryer and A.V. Paul, showing the 1900 arrangement. The 1937 layout is shown in our *Chichester to Portsmouth* album.

NEW SLIP CONNECTION INTO USE 15-5-1936

CONNECTIONS ALTERED 19-11-1933 (SEE NEXT DIAGRAM)

OOU   Out of use.
TOU   Taken out of use.
GF   Ground Frame.
LC   Level Crossing.

REMOVED } BY 1910
ADDED   }

EAST BOX 72·45 OPENED 12·6·1885

ENGINE SHED

ANGLO-AMERICAN OIL INTO USE JUNE 1915

72·60

STATION OPENED 1·7·1885

YARD BOX

JCN 00·00

WEST BOX OPENED 1·7·1885

BRANCH AREA AND JUNCTION REMODELLED 1937 (SEE NEXT DIAGRAM)

* YARD BOX REDUCED TO GF. 7·2·1932

ALTERED 1·7·1904
++++ REMOVED
– – – NEW

"A"· ENGINEER'S SIDING AND GF INTO USE 26·11·1929 SIDING ABOLISHED 19·9·1936

UP BRANCH CONVERTED TO SIDING 1·7·1904

TO EAST SOUTHSEA (ROUTE 54/09) CLOSED 8·8·1914 REMOVED 1923/24

SCISSORS CROSSINGS TOU 2·5·37

CONVERTED TO PASSENGER LINE 20·6·37

114. The original terminal buildings were replaced by the present elegant structure in 1866 which has thankfully largely survived the bombers and the redevelopers. This photograph from the early 1930s shows the extent of the enclosed high level platforms and the Greetham Street goods shed, which was closed in 1936. Only two low-level platforms now remain, the site of the others being occupied by a DIY centre and a car park. (Lens of Sutton)

116. The platform canopy, seen in the previous photograph, has been lost but the reconstruction of the road bridge but the main train sheds survive. They protect not only the passengers but numerous pigeons, roosting oblivious to the vibration of the trains. The buffet of the 16.57 to Waterloo is visible as a DEMU arrives from Salisbury on 21st July 1984. (V. Mitchell)

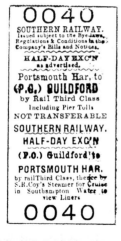

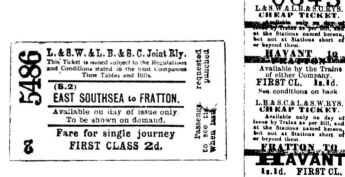

115. On the left is the beginning of the North Dockyard line, which was usable until 1978. The sharp curves create operational problems of lack of visibility and excessive gaps between coach and platform. The maximum is 17½ins at the west end of the down platform and to ensure safety a staff of five is employed on the platform. (Lens of Sutton)

PORTSMOUTH HARBOUR

117. The extension to the Harbour was opened on 2nd October 1876 and the terminus was extensively rebuilt in 1936-37 but almost completely destroyed during air raids in 1941. Platform 1 and the access siding to the Gun Wharf were repaired, but construction of the new signal box and platforms seen here had to wait until 1946. (Lens of Sutton)

118. An unusual view of the terminus devoid of trains shows that beyond platform 5 there is a siding for tankers conveying fuel oil for the Isle of Wight ferries. In the absence of run round facilities, the tanks are brought from Fratton behind a class 33 (otherwise running light as described in caption no.113) with a class 08 shunter at the rear. This performs the shunting and returns with the empties. (Lens of Sutton)

119. By 1964, steam was something less common at the Harbour and the class 4 is here relegated to a humble van train. Set no.2124 was a 2BIL, which meant **2** coaches **bil**avatoried. (D. Fereday Glenn)

Other views and details of the Portsea Island railways are to be found in the companion album *Chichester to Portsmouth*.

120. Class T9 no.30117 blows off whilst waiting to leave wih an enthusiasts railtour on 30th April 1961. Alongside is 4COR set no.3057, one of the "Nelsons" or "Pompeys" as they were affectionately known. They were the first fully gangwayed stock on the Southern and for over 30 years were synonymous with comfortable speedy travel between London and Portsmouth.
(A.E. Bennett)

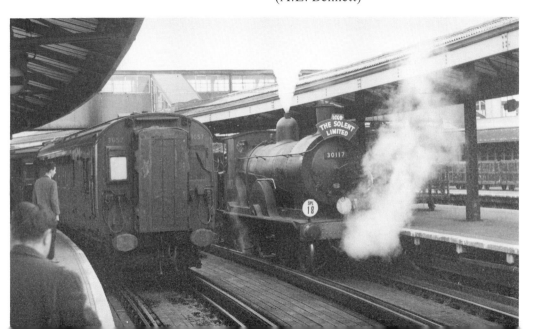

Middleton Press

Easebourne Lane, Midhurst, W Sussex. GU29 9AZ Tel: 01730 813169 Fax: 01730 812601
Email: enquiries@middletonpress.fsnet.co.uk *If books are not available from your*
local transport stockist, order direct with cheque, Visa or Mastercard, post free UK.

BRANCH LINES
Branch Line to Allhallows
Branch Line to Alton
Branch Lines around Ascot
Branch Lines to Ashburton
Branch Lines around Bodmin
Branch Line to Bude
Branch Lines around Canterbury
Branch Lines around Chard & Yeovil
Branch Line to Cheddar
Branch Lines around Cromer
Branch Line to the Derwent Valley
Branch Lines to East Grinstead
Branch Lines of East London
Branch Lines to Effingham Junction
Branch Lines around Exmouth
Branch Lines to Falmouth, Helston & St. Ives
Branch Line to Fairford
Branch Lines around Gosport
Branch Line to Hayling
Branch Lines to Henley, Windsor & Marlow
Branch Line to Hawkhurst
Branch Line to Ilfracombe
Branch Line to Kingsbridge
Branch Line to Kingswear
Branch Line to Lambourn
Branch Lines to Launceston & Princetown
Branch Lines to Longmoor
Branch Line to Looe
Branch Line to Lyme Regis
Branch Line to Lynton
Branch Lines around March
Branch Lines around Midhurst
Branch Line to Minehead
Branch Line to Moretonhampstead
Branch Line to Newport (IOW)
Branch Lines to Newquay
Branch Lines around North Woolwich
Branch Line to Padstow
Branch Lines around Plymouth
Branch Lines to Princes Risborough
Branch Lines to Seaton and Sidmouth
Branch Lines around Sheerness
Branch Line to Shrewsbury
Branch Line to Swanage *updated*
Branch Line to Tenterden
Branch Lines around Tiverton
Branch Lines to Torrington
Branch Lines to Tunbridge Wells
Branch Line to Upwell
Branch Lines of West London
Branch Lines of West Wiltshire
Branch Lines around Weymouth
Branch Lines around Wimborne
Branch Lines around Wisbech

NARROW GAUGE
Branch Line to Lynton
Branch Lines around Portmadoc 1923-46
Branch Lines around Porthmadog 1954-94
Branch Line to Southwold
Douglas to Port Erin
Douglas to Peel
Kent Narrow Gauge
Northern France Narrow Gauge
Romneyrail
Southern France Narrow Gauge
Sussex Narrow Gauge
Surrey Narrow Gauge
Swiss Narrow Gauge
Two-Foot Gauge Survivors
Vivarais Narrow Gauge

SOUTH COAST RAILWAYS
Ashford to Dover
Bournemouth to Weymouth
Brighton to Worthing
Eastbourne to Hastings
Hastings to Ashford
Portsmouth to Southampton
Ryde to Ventnor
Southampton to Bournemouth

SOUTHERN MAIN LINES
Basingstoke to Salisbury
Bromley South to Rochester
Crawley to Littlehampton
Dartford to Sittingbourne
East Croydon to Three Bridges
Epsom to Horsham
Exeter to Barnstaple
Exeter to Tavistock
Faversham to Dover
London Bridge to East Croydon
Orpington to Tonbridge
Tonbridge to Hastings
Salisbury to Yeovil
Sittingbourne to Ramsgate
Swanley to Ashford
Tavistock to Plymouth
Three Bridges to Brighton
Victoria to Bromley South
Victoria to East Croydon
Waterloo to Windsor
Waterloo to Woking
Woking to Portsmouth
Woking to Southampton
Yeovil to Exeter

EASTERN MAIN LINES
Barking to Southend
Ely to Kings Lynn
Ely to Norwich
Fenchurch Street to Barking
Hitchin to Peterborough
Ilford to Shenfield
Ipswich to Saxmundham
Liverpool Street to Ilford
Saxmundham to Yarmouth
Tilbury Loop

WESTERN MAIN LINES
Bristol to Taunton
Didcot to Banbury
Didcot to Swindon
Ealing to Slough
Exeter to Newton Abbot
Newton Abbot to Plymouth
Newbury to Westbury
Paddington to Ealing
Paddington to Princes Risborough
Plymouth to St. Austell
Princes Risborough to Banbury
Reading to Didcot
Slough to Newbury
St. Austell to Penzance
Swindon to Bristol
Taunton to Exeter
Westbury to Taunton

MIDLAND MAIN LINES
St. Albans to Bedford
Euston to Harrow & Wealdstone
St. Pancras to St. Albans

COUNTRY RAILWAY ROUTES
Abergavenny to Merthyr
Andover to Southampton
Bath to Evercreech Junction
Bath Green Park to Bristol
Burnham to Evercreech Junction
Cheltenham to Andover
Croydon to East Grinstead
Didcot to Winchester
East Kent Light Railway
Fareham to Salisbury
Frome to Bristol
Guildford to Redhill
Reading to Basingstoke
Reading to Guildford
Redhill to Ashford
Salisbury to Westbury
Stratford upon Avon to Cheltenham
Strood to Paddock Wood
Taunton to Barnstaple
Wenford Bridge to Fowey
Westbury to Bath
Woking to Alton
Yeovil to Dorchester

GREAT RAILWAY ERAS
Ashford from Steam to Eurostar
Clapham Junction 50 years of change
Festiniog in the Fifties
Festiniog in the Sixties
Festiniog 50 years of enterprise
Isle of Wight Lines 50 years of change
Railways to Victory 1944-46
Return to Blaenau 1970-82
SECR Centenary album
Talyllyn 50 years of change
Wareham to Swanage 50 years of change
Yeovil 50 years of change

LONDON SUBURBAN RAILWAYS
Caterham and Tattenham Corner
Charing Cross to Dartford
Clapham Jn. to Beckenham Jn.
Crystal Palace (HL) & Catford Loop
East London Line
Finsbury Park to Alexandra Palace
Holbourn Viaduct to Lewisham
Kingston and Hounslow Loops
Lewisham to Dartford
Lines around Wimbledon
Liverpool Street to Chingford
London Bridge to Addiscombe
Mitcham Junction Lines
North London Line
South London Line
West Croydon to Epsom
West London Line
Willesden Junction to Richmond
Wimbledon to Beckenham
Wimbledon to Epsom

STEAMING THROUGH
Steaming through Cornwall
Steaming through the Isle of Wight
Steaming through Kent
Steaming through West Hants

TRAMWAY CLASSICS
Aldgate & Stepney Tramways
Barnet & Finchley Tramways
Bath Tramways
Brighton's Tramways
Bristol's Tramways
Burton & Ashby Tramways
Camberwell & W.Norwood Tramways
Clapham & Streatham Tramways
Croydon's Tramways
Dover's Tramways
East Ham & West Ham Tramways
Edgware and Willesden Tramways
Eltham & Woolwich Tramways
Embankment & Waterloo Tramways
Exeter & Taunton Tramways
Fulwell - Home to Trams, Trolleys and Buses
Great Yarmouth Tramways
Greenwich & Dartford Tramways
Hammersmith & Hounslow Tramway
Hampstead & Highgate Tramways
Hastings Tramways
Holborn & Finsbury Tramways
Ilford & Barking Tramways
Kingston & Wimbledon Tramways
Lewisham & Catford Tramways
Liverpool Tramways 1. Eastern Routes
Liverpool Tramways 2. Southern Routes
Liverpool Tramways 3. Northern Routes
Maidstone & Chatham Tramways
Margate to Ramsgate
North Kent Tramways
Norwich Tramways
Reading Tramways
Seaton & Eastbourne Tramways
Shepherds Bush & Uxbridge Tramways
Southend-on-sea Tramways
South London Line Tramways 1903-3
Southwark & Deptford Tramways
Stamford Hill Tramways
Twickenham & Kingston Tramways
Victoria & Lambeth Tramways
Waltham Cross & Edmonton Tramways
Walthamstow & Leyton Tramways
Wandsworth & Battersea Tramways

TROLLEYBUS CLASSICS
Croydon Trolleybuses
Derby Trolleybuses
Hastings Trolleybuses
Huddersfield Trolleybuses
Maidstone Trolleybuses
Portsmouth Trolleybuses
Reading Trolleybuses
Woolwich & Dartford Trolleybuses

WATERWAY ALBUMS
Kent and East Sussex Waterways
London to Portsmouth Waterway
West Sussex Waterways

MILITARY BOOKS
Battle over Portsmouth
Battle over Sussex 1940
Blitz over Sussex 1941-42
Bombers over Sussex 1943-45
Bognor at War
Military Defence of West Sussex
Military Signals from the South Coast
Secret Sussex Resistance
Surrey Home Guard

OTHER RAILWAY BOOKS
Index to all Middleton Press stations
Industrial Railways of the South-East
South Eastern & Chatham Railways
London Chatham & Dover Railway
London Termini - Past and Proposed
War on the Line (SR 1939-45)

BIOGRAPHY
Garraway Father & Son